Baldur's Gate 3: Guide to the game Tips, Tricks, Strategies to Become a Pro Player

Copyright by Richard Rivera

Contents

INTRODUCTION

If you're just beginning your journey in Baldur's Gate 3, you may have already noticed its vast scope, making it easy to get confused—especially with the added complexity of D&D elements. Navigating through various aspects of the game, such as changing party members, deciding the fate of an entire village, and weighing the advantages and disadvantages of saving a troublesome intellect devourer, can be quite challenging.

This guide aims to assist you with fundamental instructions and highlight some easily overlooked side quests. Additionally, it provides guidance for making critical storyline choices within Baldur's Gate 3. Let's dive right in, but be cautious of spoilers, of course.

Desecrated Tomb

The Defiled Tomb is your starting point in Lords of the Fallen, where you'll be introduced to the basic controls and mechanics of the game. We'll take you step-by-step through your first area, giving you an overview of the enemies you'll encounter and any important items you might find.

Once you've chosen your class and created your character, you'll awaken in the Blighted Tomb, ready to begin your journey. A mysterious stranger gives you a blue glowing lamp and asks you to meet him later.

Start by climbing the stairs directly in front of you. When you reach the top, at first it appears to be a dead end with branches covering the windows. Turn left and you'll see wooden crates and coffins partially blocking the entrance to the next area. Break through them and head into the next room to face your first enemy and get the chance to test your fighting skills.

Click left mouse button or RB to quickly attack. Click or hold the right mouse button or RT for a heavy attack.

The enemy in this room will use a wooden cross and his attacks will be slow. It would take time for him to prepare for the attack and then raise the cross above his head and slam it into the ground.

After defeating this enemy, continue through the ruins and you will reach a stone door leading to the right. Before you go here, look to the left and you will see a golden glow indicating that you need to pick up an item. Go down to the body in the water and take the item - the skull.

Now go back up the slope and through the stone doorway to continue on your way. In the next room you will be given a guide on how to lock on to targets and switch between them.

Use the mouse wheel/middle mouse button to lock onto your target. Or use the right stick on a controller. Then move the right stick left and right or press Z and X to switch between targets.

There are two enemies waiting for you in this room, just like the first one you encountered in the Desecrated Tomb. Their slow and powerful attacks give you time to try out switching between two targets and dodging their attacks.

After clearing this area of two enemies, go up the small stairs. It's on the left side of the statue and in the far right corner if you're looking at the room from where you originally entered it.

You will then be asked to test your running and jumping skills. Press the left stick or V to run up the stairs, then once you reach the top, fight your way through the spikes next to the skeleton to open a hallway.

You will then be asked to run and jump over the gap in the hallway in front of you. However, if you fall, you can pick up one of the armor shades available in the game.

Press the left stick and A on the controller or V and F on the keyboard. Exit the room and you'll be back in the room with the statue where you just fought two targets. Go up the stairs again, then run and jump over the gap to reach the other side. When you reach the end of the corridor, you will turn left and at the other end you will meet an enemy who uses ranged attacks, which will lead to a tutorial on how to dodge the attacks.

Use Spacebar to dodge. Or use B on the controller. Dodge twice to get out of the way of oncoming attacks.

Once you have dodged the incoming fireballs and managed to reach the enemy responsible, kill him to continue. Climb the stairs to get up and out, and grab the stone at the top.

After learning how to open and use your inventory, it's your turn to try your hand at ranged combat.

Proceeding further into the ruins, you will see a lone enemy under a hanging corpse. This is another enemy that wields a wooden cross and attacks slowly, but you don't have to worry about that as you're encouraged to try fighting it from a distance. Once you've dealt with the enemy below, use a ranged weapon to hit the hanging skeleton and knock down the object, which is a wooden cross.

Go right and you will reach a door where you will see a group of moths floating outside. This points to a place where you can use your lantern to leave the Axiom and enter the Umbral realm of the dead. Pick up your lantern and use it to peer into the Umbral.

The door will turn into a door with an eye looking at you, but the Dark Entity will not allow you to go further.

Turn left and go to the iron gate. Use your flashlight when you get there to see the gate disappear, allowing you to go through it.

When you enter this section, an enemy will immediately be waiting for you. Kill him, then go left to learn about attack combos and take out two additional enemies ahead. Continue past the rubble and into a red-hued hallway where Healing and the role of Sanguinarix will be explained.

Continuing along this section will lead you to another dead end with a broken bridge and a pond. If you look into the Umbral, you will see two arms that almost connect, allowing you to reach the other side. However, if you try to walk through them by simply shining a lamp on the way, you will fall and Umbral will disappear. Instead, you need to infiltrate the Umbral to get to the next section.

Once you've crossed the bridge, climb over the two arms and grab the items from the body on the other side. Jump down and to the left, then aim for the blue glowing body in the left corner. This is an obstacle to Soul Torture, and you will need to perform a Soul Torture move to remove the spikes blocking your path.

Jump down to the lower ledge, then down to the right to continue down the path. Now that you've learned how to overcome obstacles, you'll also learn how to hit targets and manipulate their movements to your advantage. Once you've practiced with the target at the bottom of this area, go up the slope to the left, starting with the area that looks like a hand.

Here your path will again be blocked by a pile of thorns and a body suspended from them. Target it and use Soul Flay on it to remove the spikes. By this point, you've probably already used up your charges, so you'll need to siphon new ones from enemies and growths to replenish your charges.

Follow the path to the next enemy and learn about Wither, which will affect your health while you're in Umbral. Kill the first enemy, then go left to see two enemies under a statue. Rid the area of them, then target the statue and use your abilities on it to make it drop an item, which is the Holy Quintessence.

Turn right and launch yourself from the top ledge onto the enemy below, performing an air attack. Face the bone ramp and walk up it to practice controlling enemy movements with your abilities.

When you get to the top, go up the stairs. Go into the corridor and you will see that it is blocked by spikes. Go outside through the hole on the right and use your abilities on the target hanging outside. This will remove the spikes and allow you to continue down the corridor. This will not only remove the spikes blocking the corridor, but you will also see a cutscene showing the door blocked by the entity earlier. Killing the last target will now mean that this door will be open for you.

At the end of the corridor you will be greeted by the remains. They can be used to exit the Umbral and return you to the Axiom. As you progress, you will see them scattered throughout Mournstead, and only in these places will you be able to return to Axiom.

Once back in Axiom, the path will open and you can go down the stairs on the left. You'll encounter another enemy closer to the bottom and can practice how to attack from higher ledges. Then just jump down and you'll be back at the door you saw before. Open it and you'll complete the Defiled Tomb and Lords of the Fallen tutorial by entering the Forlorn Red Grove.

Abandoned Red Grove

The Abandoned Red Grove is the second location you'll visit on your journey through Mournstead. After completing the Defiled Tomb tutorial, it's time to head to the game's first boss fight. In this section of our Lords of the Fallen walkthrough, we'll take you step-by-step through this new area and provide information on where to collect items, the enemies you'll encounter, and tips for defeating the bosses you'll encounter.

When you leave the Desecrated Tomb through the newly opened door and head outside, you will find yourself in the Forlorn Red Grove. The first thing you'll see when you step into the open space is the statue on the left, surrounded by blue butterflies. This is your very first bonfire in the game - Ranik's Remains. Activate the remains and you will receive a Dried Moth.

Use of remains

You'll use the remains around Mournstead as checkpoints to rest and replenish your supplies, upgrade your character, and as you unlock more of these points you'll be able to use them to travel to different areas. When you die in Umbral, you will return to the last bonfire you used.

From Ranik's Remains, go left and look for the golden glow of objects that lie near the body under the tree. Collect them and you will receive Tacitus' Diary and the Map of Mournstead. If you open the menu now, you will be able to see the Journal tab. Here you can find all your cards throughout the game.

On the map of Mournstead you will see five red lighthouses. These are the five beacons that you will have to visit throughout the game and eventually extinguish in order to ease the darkness of Adyr and bring light back to Mournstead.

Continue down the slope and you will enter an arena where a lone figure awaits you in the center. It's time for your first boss battle in the game!

Blocking and parrying training

If you block attacks, your health bar will change and part of your health will turn grey. This will be your withered health. If you then successfully attack an enemy without taking damage, you will be able to regain that health. However, if you get hit, you will lose all your health, highlighted in grey. If you manage to parry an attack, this will mean that your health bar will become smaller and you will affect the enemy's position.

The enemy's position can be seen by the circle that appears when you target them. You'll see a full circle at first and will slowly fade away every time you parry a blow. Once the enemy's position is reduced enough, you can perform a kick, heavy attack, or other parry to knock the enemy down. The pose circle will turn red and you can perform a Hard Strike by pressing the attack button to deal significant damage.

When you enter the arena, Holy Bulwark Otto will rush towards you. This fight serves as a tutorial for the boss fights you'll encounter throughout the game, so it's a good opportunity to practice blocking and parrying attacks. These challenging fights feature enemies with increased health bars that will hinder your progress through the main story.

Boss Fight - Otto's Holy Bulwark

Due to two-handed heavy weapons, Holy Bulwark Otto's movement and attacks are quite slow. He prefers overhead strikes and does them quite often, raising his weapon high above his head and slamming it into the ground. He takes a moment to recover before he launches his next attack, creating ample opportunities for you to retaliate.

In addition to this move, he will simply swing his heavy weapon around. These attacks can be easily dodged, but are also good practice for blocking/parrying. If he manages to hit you with his weapon, you will suffer bleed damage. This bleed gauge can be seen above your health bar and will increase with each hit. If it fills up, you will begin to bleed and your health bar will deplete until the effect wears off.

Every now and then, Holy Bulwark Otto spins his mace around his head before slamming it downwards, with a slight lunge that propels him forward. Be sure to dodge this strike or try to block it, but run towards the boss as soon as he finishes his attack, as he will take a little longer to pull his weapon out of the ground, leaving you with a chance to stun him.

One move you should watch out for that can end a fight quickly is when he raises his left hand and rushes towards you. If he catches you, he will grab you by the throat and use his mace to hit you in the body, significantly draining your health bar and sending you flying.

When you defeat Holy Bulwark Otto, a cutscene will begin and the Reaper of Light will descend, replacing the first boss in battle.

Boss Fight - Reaper of Light

The Reaper of Light can be fought and won in this fight, but at such a low level it will be incredibly difficult. The goal is to die to the Reaper of Light here, but skilled players will be able to defeat him.

If you die to the Reaper of Light, you will be reborn. Return to the arena and restore your Energy. Go behind the tree and take the path to the right first. You will reach a dead end, and even in Umbral you will not be able to get past the door that appears. Pick up the item here (Flaid Skin), then turn around and walk in the opposite direction until you see an enemy at the edge.

Here you will learn how to remove parasites from your enemies. Remove the parasite and destroy the enemy to be able to pick up the item next to it, which is a map. It may also seem like a dead end if you're not already in Umbral. If you are in Axiom, your lantern will start to glow and spectral ribbons will start coming out of it, and there will be a wall of moths at the edge. This is your sign that you will need to go to Umbral to continue, and that the path can only be unlocked in this world.

Use your abilities to target the soul hanging from the cliff and pull it towards you so you can reach the other side. Walk up the bone ramp to reach another ruins checkpoint (Hannelore's Remains) and you'll be greeted by a mysterious man called the Iron Traveler.

If you want to leave the Umbral Realm and return to Axiom at any time, you can relax by the fire.

Stay here in Umbral, or return to it if you've been resting. You will need to be in the Umbral to see the memory that appears in the next section. Go to the left of the fire and jump down to see what looks like a soul on its knees.

Use your abilities to extract memories from the soul and review the memory. They will show you fragments of the past. Go left to collect 3 Small Holy Salts.

Go back, then go left and towards the trees. This will allow you to not only collect the item here, but also bypass the enemy that awaits at the end of this section. Take the items and then destroy the enemy. Be prepared to fight two more as soon as you leave this path.

Continue along this path and you will see a scarecrow on the left that will allow you to exit the Umbral. Immediately on the right, you will see a small alley. There are three enemies hiding here, but you'll likely only notice one.

Kill them, then go to the next area where you will see a corpse hanging from a tree with some kind of item. Don't go straight to the item and body, instead go through the first gate on the left where you will see another item glow. At the far end of this area, an enemy is waiting for you, but be careful when walking towards him, as another enemy will appear from the wooden wall on the left. You can attack them by breaking through the wooden wall and destroying them. Once this area is clear, pick up the Broken Sword.

As you approach the tree, look for an enemy on the hill who will throw fireballs at you. Take him out first so you can focus on the two surrounding the tree. In addition, here you will find another creature that can throw fireballs at you, which has a parasite attached to it. He will walk up and down the enemy's right side on a raised platform. Use your Shadow Lamp to kill the parasite and leave the creature vulnerable to attacks. Once this area is clear, hit the corpse on the tree to drop a Pilgrim's Robe and a Pilgrim's Skirt.

Then go behind the tree to the left. You'll find another enemy waiting for you just outside the iron gate on the right. Once you get rid of it, go left to the wooden crates. All of them can be smashed to reveal enemies hiding behind them, as well as items from the body in the left corner, namely 2 ammo bags and 2 small clusters of mana stones.

Now go to Umbral and head towards the exit of this area where you found the enemy with the parasite. Look to the right as you head towards the stairs and you will see an enemy with a heavy sword and an item near the barn door. This enemy can be a challenge early in the game, with its fire attacks, projectiles, and heavy sword strikes, so take your time or rush past it.

Take the item (Shield of the Orian Preacher) and go right to go up the stairs. Here you will be able to cross a bone bridge to reach the roof of a thatched house, and at the top you will see a corpse with an item. Shoot it down, then jump down to the other side to fight two more creatures and collect more items in the area, as well as the one you shot down. Items you can collect in this area include the Mangler's Raw Ax and 2 Skulls.

When you're done, go up the wooden slope on the right and return to the stairs leading up and out. You can leave Umbral here to return to Axiom and continue your climb upward. When you reach the wooden planks, you will find two enemies hiding behind them. Once they are killed, continue up the stairs and find the enemy hiding on the left by the door.

At the top you will see an enemy looking into the distance. Here you will be given a guide on how to stun enemies and attack them from behind. Once you do this, go to the left of where the enemy was standing and break the boards. Here you can pick up 3 unripe berries. Now continue left and go up the next set of stairs.

Once you reach the top of the stairs, you will see a door. It's locked for now, so go towards it, but turn left. Once hidden, you can see the next bonfire - the Remains of Marco the Axe. Rest if necessary and use this checkpoint.

Enter Umbral and look at the door again, but go left and look down. Here you can use the lantern to lower a ledge from which you can jump down. Go down to the right and use your abilities on the target in the center, surrounded by stone souls, to pick up the Shadow Eye of Devoted Eliard. Then go to the right of this statue to find another growth that you can use to get two Dark Purifications.

When you're done, go up the bone stairs behind the statue. Jump off the boards, then go back and climb up to the remains to return to the Axiom. Stand in front of the door (with your back to the slope you can climb up from) and go left to continue your journey.

To the right you will see another body suspended with some kind of object. Attack him once you've cleared the area to get the Miner's Ring. Near the body you will see a broken bridge. Look to your left to see where you need to go, as you won't be able to cross the bridge yet.

Follow the slope down where you will see that it is flooded. Use the lamp to enter Umbral and continue on your way. You will reach a point where there is a corridor going off to the left with egg-shaped vessels lining it. Shortly before this, you will be able to pick up a bag of ammunition and a lot of manastone from the body.

Go left down the hallway and as you go through it you will have to fight some ghouls to get to the other side. When you do this, go right and find a statue with an object hanging from it. Shoot him down to get a Pilgrim's Hood and a Pilgrim's Bandage, then turn around and go back. Look at the wall you just passed and you will see a bone staircase leading up.

At the top of this section there will be butchers wandering around. You can exit Umbral and return to Axiom here. Then go left to knock down the plank and build a bridge for a shortcut.

Once done, go right and continue forward until you see fire in the distance. If you go right you'll be back at the statue, so just go left. Go upstairs and take 3 items from the body. Then go right and jump left to go inside the building.

Here you will meet the Iron Traveler, who will explain how the remains seeds work. Use them to create a temporary fire where you can rest. Now go up the stairs to exit the building. Climb the stairs up until you reach the ground on fire.

Head right to see a fight between different creatures and clear them out to find some items. You then need to head to the building ruins on the left for the next boss fight.

Boss Fight - Pieta

At the beginning of the fight with Pieta, she will approach you in a cautious stance. Her attacks will range from using her sword for normal attacks to Radiance beams. When she uses her sword, she attacks with ranged attacks. You can expect them when she starts swaying. They can be dodged, parried, or blocked. She usually swings her sword 2-3 times before stopping. At these moments she will be vulnerable to attack. In addition to these consecutive attacks, she will also jump, swing her sword, and slam it on the ground. The cooldown on these attacks will be slightly longer, giving you a better chance of landing a hit.

When it comes to attacking with Radiance beams, it will only take her a second to charge the beam and release it. You'll know when she's about to do this because she holds her sword right in front of you and a glow will immediately begin to emanate from the edge of the sword. In addition to this, she will use a sword attack that will follow you, creating a path from Pieta towards you. Both of these attacks can be dodged and the damage completely avoided.

Second phase of the battle

In the second stage, she will fly to one end of the battlefield and hover in the air for a moment. This will give you enough time to move away from her oncoming attack. To do this, you need to stand on both sides of the arena, avoiding the middle. Soon she will rush forward in a shining arc, cutting the path, and a shower of golden arrows will fall from above. At this point, Pieta will be able to repeat this attack, and sometimes change it by introducing golden copies of himself into the fight. When this happens, you should consider the battlefield as three lanes, one of which is safe, and two additional ones are covered by clone attacks.

Once you defeat Pieta, go to the Umbra if you haven't already. You will be able to read the memories on Pieta's body to gain a special "Pieta Memory" as well as two "Dark Purifications".

Skyrest Bridge

Skyrest Bridge is the third area you'll come to on your journey through Mournstead. After defeating Pieta, you will gain access to a new area and will be able to catch up with the mysterious stranger from the very beginning of the game. In this section of our Lords of the Fallen walkthrough, we'll take you step-by-step through this new area and include information on how to deal with enemies, where to collect items, and we'll also give tips on defeating the bosses you'll encounter.

As soon as you enter the Skyrest Bridge, a cutscene will begin in which you will be reunited with the person from the beginning of the game who gave you the Shadow Lantern. This area will be your main hub in the game, where you can upgrade your gear, find keys to access hidden routes around Mournstead, and complete some side quests, among other things.

When you first enter this area, you can talk to several people waiting for you, but you also need to go back and activate the bonfire - Etrig's Remains. As for those you'll find here, here's a quick overview of who they are and what they have to offer you.

Ecster Dunmire

Ecster Dunmire will be the first person you see as you walk towards the back of the Skyrest Bridge. He will explain that he is the Head of the Dark Crusaders, and he is tasked with cleansing Mournstead of the corruption caused by Adyr.

Pieta

You can find her standing to the left of the remains behind the bridge. Now that the Pieta has been cleansed of corruption, it is no longer your enemy. Pieta will introduce himself as a member of the Sacred Guardians. In exchange for Holy Quintessions, Pieta will upgrade your Sanguinaryx, giving it extra charges and greater effectiveness when it comes to healing.

At this point you should have Holy Quintessence from the Defiled Tomb so you can increase the charges from 3 to 4.

Molhu

Opposite the Pieta there is a staircase. If you are in the Axiom and go up it, you will see an empty room. You will need to enter the Umbra to find Molhu, who lives in this part of the area. Molhu is responsible for upgrading your Shadow Lantern and can do so in exchange for Anti-Diluven Chisels. In addition to upgrading your lantern, you can also insert Shadow Eyes into her.

If you followed our walkthrough, you picked up Devoted Eliard's Dark Eye in the Forsaken Red Grove. This particular Shadow Eye will give you +15% Terror Resistance and an extra charge of Soul Torture, so it's worth using for now.

Finally, Molhu can also give you access to special equipment and armor that can only be obtained after defeating bosses. At this point you should have Memories of the Pietà, but you will need the Chalice of Revelations from Pilgrim's Descent before you can trade memories for items.

After you defeat the boss, you will need to impale his body. This will allow you to see special memories. If you have a Memory, you can give it to Molch to gain access to unique weapons, spells, and armor. To purchase these items, you will need to use Shadow Scrapers.

Temple of the Rotten Mother

To the left of Molhu is the Temple of the Rotten Mother. This is another object that can only be interacted with while in the Umbral. This location is only available when you are online. When you are online, you can exchange eyeballs for other items.

Stomund, captain of the Fidelis

To the right of the Remains you will find Stomund. He intends to restore order and believes that the Dark Crusader and the Shadow Lantern are a necessary evil to accomplish this task. Once you have exhausted your dialogue options with him, you will be able to trade with him. In addition to a variety of equipment and armor, Stomund also offers the Key to the Pilgrimage Site for 9000 Energy.

Eustace and Nathaniel

Behind Stomund there is a corridor that will lead you to another room. Go down the stairs and you will see two people. Both are members of Fidelis. The first one standing by the camera on the left is Eustace, and the one standing by the statue is Nathaniel.

Temple of Orius

Nathaniel stands near the Shrine of Orius, which you can interact with in the same way as the Shrine of the Rotten Mother. To use it, you need to be online and logged in. You will be able to obtain various items by using this shrine.

Andreas

To the right of Stomund is another staircase that will take you out of the main building. Once you go down it, you will see someone standing on a ledge. This is Andreas of Ebb, a nobleman who wants you to hand over the Shadow Lamp. It doesn't offer much at this point, just dialogue about how you'll suffer a terrible fate while carrying the lamp.

Leave the main building

Continue down the stairs after speaking with Andreas to exit the main building of the location and begin your journey to the pilgrimage site. Just before the stairs, look to the right and pick up the Old Mournstead Spear.

Go up the stairs and continue along the wooden platform until you see a man standing on the right. This is Teh-Ihir. Exhaust all dialogue options, then continue along the platform until it reaches a dead end.

Jump down to the left and be careful of the hiding enemies who are ready to attack you from behind. Here you will encounter soldiers and creatures using ranged Radiance attacks, so go across the first platform and look for the item to the left of the body. This is a new card.

If you're in Umbral, you'll also see a huge skeleton just behind this platform. Look at the end of the bone bridge on the right to find a target that you can impact to get the item.

Continue down the stairs where you will see a scarecrow. Then go left and down the next set of stairs to reach a large wooden platform and open area. Once you enter, look to your right to see the building you need to enter.

If you stay on the platform to clear the area, you'll need to watch out for the many soldiers hiding behind the wooden crates and look up to see creatures attacking you from several raised platforms. Look at the first section on the left when you enter this place. At the edge you can find useful items.

After clearing the area, enter the building. Be sure to be in the Umbral so you can use your abilities and see the Memories fragment. Then go up the stairs and go right to activate a new bonfire - Chabuya's Remains.

Go up the stairs opposite the fire, and then go up the second one. Go to the end of the corridor, then turn right and go through the beam. On the other side, turn right again and enter Umbral. This will open the grate on the right and show you a body to search.

Now follow the corridor in the opposite direction and you will come to a ladder leading down and some crates on the other side of the gap. Break the crates and go into the body chamber to find a grenade.

Go down the stairs and start walking in the opposite direction. While in Umbral, you will see someone standing on the second level looking down at the chapel. Talk to him, then continue left. Continue past the next set of stairs to go through an invisible gate to the platform below. It is located just above the bonfire and contains 3x Bleed Resistance Balm that you can obtain.

You will need to go back (you should also rest to return to the Axiom), then go down the second stairs and get to the lower floor of the Chapel. Enter the chapel and you will see two believers near the statue. There is also an item here that you can pick up: Bloody Aspergillum.

Clear the area of the two parishioners, then go right. You'll see a figure waiting for you, and once you get close, the next boss battle will begin.

Boss Fight - Wicker Sister Dilit

Wicker Sister Delyth will begin to approach you when you reach the stairs. Her health bar will be blue until she gets to the top of the stairs herself, so you won't be able to attack until you remove the parasite that can be found to the right. While she's getting closer, you'll have plenty of time to fire off some long-range shots.

She then usually starts the fight by winding up her mace and sending out a tornado that causes both bleeding and Radiance damage. When it reaches you, the tornado will explode, creating a large affected area. Since it explodes whenever it hits something, you can avoid this attack by throwing yourself behind the pillars and the tornado will explode on impact, leaving you unharmed.

In addition to these ranged attacks, Wicker Sister Delith will use her mace and strike in rapid succession. They can be blocked or parried, but if you're good at dodging, they can be avoided. Once this move is completed, you will have a moment where she will stop and be open to attack.

Second phase of the battle

When her health bar is between two-thirds and one-half depleted, she will transform and create a glowing ring around herself. Her attacks will be faster and stronger as she charges longer, and her weapon will have a slight delay, making it harder for you to time your parry. During these sequential attacks, she will hit several times and then spin around and perform a 360 degree attack.

After defeating the Sister, you will receive a seed, the Wicker Sister's Flail, and the Wicker Sister's Helm. If you're not in Umbral yet, you need to check it out. After leaving the location, look to the right and you will see a niche with a body from which you can get Holy Quintessence.

Once you have collected everything, leave the area and go up the stairs to begin exploring the pilgrimage site.

Place of pilgrimage

This is the fourth location you'll come to on your journey through Mournstead. Now that Wicker Sister Delith has been defeated, you can continue your ascent.

When you enter this area, you will be greeted by a bleak landscape with rain and lightning falling on wooden platforms. Before you continue, it's good to know that this whole climb will be dangerous, not only because of the enemies, but also because of the many platforms and ledges that you can fall from.

From this first platform there are two stairs, one going down and the other going up. If you look to the left, you will also see an item on the ledge. Head there and you and the item will fall onto the lower ledge. Take the item, then enter the Umbral.

What looked like a dead end will now turn into a bone bridge. Run and jump across the bridge, then approach the body on the other side, on the edge of the platform. Grab the Rending Knife, then return to the first platform and climb the stairs to reach the top.

Here you need to enter the cave and go to a room where there is a door on the left and some shady flower beds where you can create a checkpoint. We recommend that you use a seed here to create a control point.

Key to the place of pilgrimage

You won't be able to enter the door on the left until you get the Pilgrim's Place Key from Stomund. It costs 9000 Energy.

Continue to the left of the door and exit into the street. You'll see how small the platforms are now as you start to climb, but just as enemies can push you away, you can also push them off ledges. Don't forget that using abilities also allows you to control enemies, so you can use this to your advantage.

Before you start going up the stairs, you'll need to re-enter the Umbral (if you didn't stay there) to collect a few more items. To the left of the platforms you will see another bone bridge. Go up it and jump over the gap to collect the salt, then go down it and jump over to search the body, this will allow you to find a hollow bow and pulsating arrows.

If you planted a seed, return and rest to begin your ascent in Axiom. When you first start going up this path, look for an enemy on the raised platform to the right and get rid of him. This will make climbing easier and you won't have to worry about ranged attacks. There will be two worshipers on the right at the first staircase, and then another as you go up the second staircase.

However, the most important thing to focus on as you climb the second flight of stairs is the large enemy with the spiked helmet. He will rush at you, swinging his arms to attack and slamming his head down to hit you with his spiked helmet. Use the platforms to your advantage and try to lure him to the edge while dodging to the right as he lunges at you. Hopefully this will push him over the edge so you don't have to fight him. Once you clear the area of these enemies, you can pick up the item that was near the only worshiper on the second staircase. These are small fragments of deralium.

If you try to walk to the end of the path, you will see that the board is raised and you will not be able to continue. Instead, you need to take the stairs on the right. Once you reach the top, first turn right to collect the simple shield from the body at the end. Now go left, enter the Umbral and go to the edge. Use your abilities to move the bone platform towards you and get to the other side.

Look up and to the left to target enemies that will use ranged attacks and destroy them to make the climb easier. Then look at the stairs going down to the left, go down them and approach the plank to knock it down and create a shortcut. Turn around and look to the left to see another staircase going down. This will lead you to a small platform where you can grab a Common Oriya Prayer from the table.

Now go back up both stairs to continue. Watch out for another enemy with a spiked helmet hiding just behind the small board that will lead you to the next section. Clear this area and before using the scarecrow to return to the Axiom, go left and behind the wooden structure and stairs.

Here you can go down the stairs. Then run in the opposite direction from the stairs and you will find a body hidden on the left. Search it to get a Corrupted Ring. Now go up the stairs and return to the scarecrow. Use it to return to the Axiom and go up the stairs.

Kill the two enemies above, then look to the left to see swinging platforms. You will need to run and jump over two hanging platforms to get to the next section. Be careful of the enemies on the second platform that use ranged attacks (if you haven't already destroyed them), as they have a parasite attached to them that you will need to destroy first. Pick up the bell staff next to this enemy once you get rid of it, then jump over to the next section and clear it. Collect the Holy Praise from the body at the altar, then go up the next set of stairs.

Go right and go up the second ladder. When you reach the top, turn around and look in the opposite direction. Here you will see a group of moths, which means you must enter the Umbral again. This will open up a bone platform going to the left. At the end you will find a body from which you can get the Ring of Holy Blood.

Now go in the opposite direction to see another enemy with a spiked helmet using ranged attacks and some more ghouls. There is a ladder here, but it's raised, so you'll have to go left and use the bones to climb up. Go as far as you can and then interact with the growth to expand the bridge. Now you will need to run and jump to overcome it.

Go up the slope, then use your abilities again to pull the platform towards you. Work your way along it to the middle, then pull it to the opposite side. Once you reach the other side, go up the slope. You will see wooden planks forming platforms through which you can reach the hand in the middle holding the object. First, go left and lower the ladder down to take a shortcut.

Now take the item from your hand which is a sword and use the planks on the left to get to the next section. As you step onto this platform, notice the entrance on the left. As you walk past him, an enemy wearing a spiked helmet will attack you from inside and try to destroy you. It also has a parasite attached to it, so before you can do any damage to it, it needs to be destroyed. If you have time to dodge, you can throw him off the ledge.

In addition to this enemy, you also need to find and deal with the one who will use ranged attacks from the platform above. Go upstairs to get rid of this creature, then search the body at the end for 4 small Deralium fragments. Jump down and go right to enter the cave.

Activate the Remains of Blind Agatha on the left. Then talk to the stranger standing opposite, named Byron. Walk behind Byron to the item to grab a new map for the next area you have to go through.

Behind Byron and the map, there is another door with a bell. It can also be opened using the Pilgrimage Key, which you can buy from Stomund.

Pilgrim's Descent

This is the fifth location you'll come to on your journey through Mournstead. Here, you will begin to descend into the dungeon. We'll guide you step-by-step through this new area and provide information on where to collect items, what enemies you'll encounter, and details on how to defeat the boss.

Opposite the Remains of Blind Agatha there is a lever. If you try to pull it, you won't be able to get anywhere because the mechanism is broken. So, you will need to follow the path to the left. When you reach the end of this path, you will immediately be greeted by a group of enemies, consisting of three worshipers and one enemy capable of attacking from a distance.

While you can jump up to them fairly easily, you'll want to watch out for the second group of enemies on the left, across the wooden walkway. There are two enemies here that will immediately start hitting you with ranged attacks. The rest are parishioners who can be destroyed without much difficulty.

After passing through the passage, on the left you will see a doorway that will lead you further. However, if you look to the right, you will see a pond and stairs. You need to go to Umbral to climb the stairs.

Follow the path to the top, where you will be met by an enemy spitting poison, as well as several ordinary ghouls. Clear the area, then look for the body on the left. From it you will receive Rosamund's Shadow Eye.

Go right from here and go up the next stairs. You'll enter a room with a chest on the left, a ladder on the right, and a ledge just past the chest. First, go to the chest and open it to get Ancient Sacred Guardian Sleeves, Ancient Sacred Guardian Armor and Ancient Sacred Guardian Helmet, then go out to the ledge and take 3 Bleed Resistance Balms from the body. Now go back up the stairs (now on the left) and go outside.

Look to the right as you walk down the hallway outside to grab 3 Lesser Fire Salts from the altar. When you exit the cave, first look to the left to see a wooden structure that can be broken. Behind it you will find one of the armor shades.

There is a scarecrow at the entrance to the cave and opposite the stairs you can go down. You should switch to the Axiom to fight the crowd of enemies below, but this can be quite difficult when you are surrounded by a crowd. However, you need to return to the Umbra to pick up the stigma hanging from the cage.

Climb the stairs to the edge of this platform and find the guardian's scripture. Look back at the stairs and go right first to lower the stairs.

Then go left, crossing the wooden planks. Go to the body that is sticking out on the board on the far left and take the Ardent Penitent's Head Cage.

You need to turn around, jump down and destroy the enemy with the spiked helmet on this small platform, as well as the one who attacks you with ranged attacks. Then enter the Umbral, continue forward, cross the bone bridge that appears and fight the last two enemies who perform ranged attacks. Break the boxes on the left to reveal a body that can be used to collect 2 Ammo Bags and 2 Small Manastone Clusters.

Enter the cave behind them and you will be returned to the Remains of Blind Agatha. You should rest and level up if you have enough Energy, especially if your health and healing supplies are depleted. While going through this initial stage, look to the right and break the crates to get a Weak Energy Skull.

From the Remains of Blind Agatha, return along the path to the left and now go past the worshipers and ranged enemies. Continue up this slope to get back to where you just entered, so take out the two enemies here and then use the moving platform to jump over. Destroy the enemy with ranged attacks and get ready to attack with the spiked helmet. At the end of this passage, look down to the left and go up the long stairs to the bottom.

Go all the way until you reach the bell. Grab the 2 Ammo Bags and 2 Small Manastone Clusters from the body, then go down the stairs. When you reach the bottom, the wooden plank in front of you will break, revealing an enemy wearing a spiked helmet. Before moving further along the platform, you need to destroy this enemy first, as there is another one waiting for you on the other side. There is also an enemy at the top that will hit you with ranged attacks, as well as an enemy in the center of the platform with a parasite attached to it.

Having cleared the area, go up the small stairs to the right of the long one you went down. Grab the 2 Ammo Bags and 2 Small Mana Stone Clusters from the body in the corner, then head back down. Enter the Umbral (if you're not already there) and rip out the soul through the door blocked by the spikes and body. It will be directly opposite where the parasitic creature was sitting and to the right of the smaller staircase.

Enter the cave, then go down the first ladder. Continue further where you will see two worshipers sitting in front of the next set of stairs. Kill them and go down to the next level. Be careful when doing this because there will be several enemies here ready to attack you from a distance.

As you head towards them, on the left you will find a lever that will help make the elevator work. Clear the area on the platform next to the elevator, then you can climb up to it if you need to rest by the fire. This will now allow you to easily return back to this area.

If you've been on vacation, be sure to come back to this platform. Clear the area of enemies with ranged attacks, and the area you should eventually reach will be to their left. But first, you'll be able to hear the sound of someone talking downstairs and the repeated impacts of a hammer on metal while you're here. To find out what is causing this, you need to go down to the lower level. If you're taking the elevator down, there will be stairs on the left that you can take down.

When you get to the bottom, you'll have to fight two armored hounds and a tough enemy. After destroying a strong enemy, you can pick up the Prison Cell Key. Talk to the person behind the prison cell door and find out that her name is Gerlinda. You can give her the key to the prison cell and free her.

To the left of the prison is another door that can only be opened with the Pilgrimage Site Key. To the right of the prison, enter the small alcove and find a body, where you can collect 2 bleeding cures. Now enter Umbral and go to the end of the room opposite the prison cell. Look to the right and hit the body blocking the door. Inside you will find a chest containing the Ring of Defiance.

If you give Gerlinde the key and release her, she will disappear from the prison cell and can be found in your base. She is in the room up the stairs opposite Stomund, which used to resemble an empty workshop. Now she will be able to upgrade your weapons in exchange for fragments of energy and deralium, and will also be able to sell items.

She will also leave 4 small fragments of Deralium in the prison cell, which will be completely open when you return to it.

You can exit the Umbral using the scarecrow on the stairs and then climb up to continue on. Go right and along the platform to where you previously fought enemies with ranged attacks (past the elevator). Go down the stairs and pull the lever to call the next elevator. Go down to the very bottom of the cave and go to the next section to start the boss battle.

Boss Fight - Gentle Haverus, Mistress of the Hounds

In this fight, Gaverus will mainly focus on using ranged attacks. She will repeatedly shoot arrows at you, which you will have to dodge. Sometimes she will charge up these arrows imbued with Radiance and they will deal more damage.

If you get too close to her, she will switch to her sword and attack quickly. You can parry, block and dodge her attacks. In such cases, she tends to put her sword away after two attempts to hit you and resume attacking with her bow and arrow. She can also perform a long lunge and will take time to return the weapon, which leaves her open. If you continue to stay near her, she will throw a smoke bomb and teleport to another location in the room.

Using your ranged weapon here is a good idea, as this will prevent you from getting too close to her and getting into melee combat. However, you will also have to fight her dogs. At first, 2 to 3 dogs will be released at you, which will chase you throughout the arena. You'll have to hit each dog once to knock down its armor before you can deal any damage to it. Luckily, they can be killed in just a few hits. However, destroying the hounds does not mean that you no longer need to think about them, since they will constantly appear in the arena.

It's best to focus your attacks on Haverus rather than keep trying to destroy the hounds. You just need to focus on dodging the dog bites while you land your strikes. If you can group the hounds together and lure them towards Haverus, you can hit them all at once if you use a melee weapon.

Destroying Haverus will reward you with a Remain Seed and a Bag of Ammo. You will also receive the Sin Impaler Sword and the Sin Impaler Armlets.

Find the flame and leave the arena when you defeat Gaverus. Climb the stairs down and follow the wooden corridor. Look to the right to grab 3 Poison Resistance Balm from the body when you go outside. Further along this corridor you will come to the next bonfire - Relic of Olleren. Once you activate it, go left and outside where you will enter the Forsaken Swamp.

Abandoned swamp

This is the sixth location you'll come to on your journey through Mournstead. Once you reach the depths of Pilgrim's Descent and kill Gaverus, you will emerge. In this section of our Lords of the Fallen walkthrough, we'll take you step-by-step through this new area and provide information on where to collect items, what enemies you'll encounter, and details on how to defeat the boss.

When you go outside, you will be greeted by Teh-Ihir again. Before talking to him, turn left and go to the edge of the cliff to pick up the Abandoned Swamp Map. Now go to him. Talking to him will give you the Summon emote and you will be able to buy items from him. After a short conversation, follow the path down until you reach wooden planks covering the hole below and an item to the left.

A soldier will appear to the left so you can attack him with a ranged weapon, but there's not much point in doing so because once you get over the planks they'll drop you into the pit below. A cutscene will begin where you will be thrown onto a pile of bodies and a mass of flesh. The monster will get up and you will be thrown into the next boss fight.

Boss Fight - Flesh Congregator

What makes this boss fight a little more difficult than others is the limited area in which you can fight this giant monster. There are two places you can target your attacks: the body and the back leg. If you focus your attacks on his back leg, the boss will fall to the ground and roll over more often, giving you a chance to hit him. When the fight begins, you will see that there is a blue orb to the left of the health bar, indicating that the Flesh Congregator has a parasite that strengthens it. The first thing you need to do is destroy the parasite, which will leave the creature vulnerable.

Anything that resists poison or removes poison effects will come in handy in this fight, as the Flesh Congregator attacks with clouds of poisonous gas. Just a few hits will cause your poison gauge to reach its maximum, meaning your health will deplete over time.

Despite its size, the Flesh Congregator can move quite well, and it has several offensive moves that will cause it to rush towards you. On his right side he has an arm that is slightly larger than the others, so he can reach further with it. The creature will often quickly rush forward and slam it down to catch you. The boss will then also swing his arm from side to side, so be prepared to dodge these attacks as well.

Ranged attacks will help you in this fight as they will give you enough space to stay away from the boss while still dealing enough damage. Use the moments after the boss has performed his attacks, especially when he punches and needs time to recover, or when he is far away from you, to deal as much damage as possible.

When his health drops to almost half, you will begin to notice that the boss becomes even more aggressive. He'll start jumping up and down (like he's having a tantrum), which will knock you back and can destroy you in one hit. You will see that the poison clouds will become more frequent and the attacks will become more aggressive. How you approach this half of the fight shouldn't be any different from your strategy in the beginning, just be more prepared to dodge jumps.

When the Flesh Congregator falls, you will receive a seed and 8 Shadow Purification. You'll also need to enter the Umbral if you're not already there to clear your soul and get this boss' memory.

Return to the swamp

Once the fight is over, head outside the battlefield to resume exploring the Forsaken Swamp. You will walk down a corridor littered with skulls and see a scarecrow ahead. You'll have to switch back to Umbral soon, so there's no point in going back to Axiom unless you're low on health and have no healing charges.

Once outside, you will see a broken wooden bridge on the right, then a pond on the left. Walk to the end of the wooden bridge to collect 3 Poison Resistance Balms, then enter the Umbral to cross the water and reach the other side. As you begin to move through this new area, you will also encounter new enemies. These swampy areas contain headless bodies that can hit you with poison attacks, as well as Shuju warriors with spears. You'll need to watch out for frog-like creatures that will roll towards you, releasing clouds of poison, and enemies that throw poison bombs at you from above while standing on stilts.

As you continue, look to the right under the broken bridge to see a body with an item to collect. Grab the 3 Small Fire Salts, then continue forward to reach the other side of the bridge. At the end the path will go straight, but there is also a dead end going to the right. Go down here to collect the poison arrows, then return to the path. At the stones, right in front of the remains, you can also pick up 2 poison resistance balms. As you go further, you will again find Byron waiting for you next to Valade's Remains.

Activate the bonfire, then if you look at it you will see a path going off to the right. This will lead you to a door that is locked on the other side, but it will serve as a shortcut later when you open it. Instead, follow the torch-lit path behind Byron to continue on.

When you reach the top of the slope, just before the wooden plank forming a bridge going to the right, look to the left to grab 2 ammo bags and 2 small manastone clusters from the body on the left. Cross the bridge to the other side and go to the bottom of the slope, into the water, to collect 3 Lesser Fire Salts.

Go left across the water under the bridge with torches lighting the way. Go left again and go under the second bridge. In the distance you will see a large tree that leans to the left to find another bridge. Just before this place you need to enter Umbral and go left. Just behind the tree you can find 2 small fragments of Deralium. At the bottom of the ramp you will find a body that needs to be gutted.

Climb up the tree and grab 2 ammo bags and 2 small manastone clusters on the other side. Look for a path to the right of this item, which will lead you to a locked door near the remains. Kill the Shuju warrior here, lower the stairs to the left, then open the door to quickly return to the bonfire.

Whether you're resting or not, go back and jump down the stairs. To the right there are vines blocking the doorway. Cut them until you reach a room with two skeletons and two items. On the left you will find the Armor Shade and on the right you will find the Ring of Curse.

Exit this room and continue forward along the path until you reach a giant bonfire. If you stay close to the wall on the left, opposite the fire, you will eventually hear a buzzing sound. There are vines here that partially block the niche. Inside you will see a burning fire, a statue and an item. Talk to the woman who will ask you to free her to begin the side quest "The Petrified Woman".

Return to the fire and clear the area. Watch out for the poison-throwing enemies on stilts that will be in the water just beyond the bonfire and will follow you to attack wherever you go.

If you look at the map of the Abandoned Swamp, you will see that you need to go under a bridge made of wood and continue along the path to find two statues that form another bridge. To do this, you need to go to the left side of the fire and follow the path.

When you cross, there will be a scarecrow on the left that you can use to return to the Axiom. When you cross the bridge with the statues, you need to turn left and walk to the end of this path. At the end you will see another body of water with creatures on stilts throwing poison and a wooden bridge to the left. However, it gets blocked as the board rises.

Enter the Umbral, then go down and go through the hole. Turn right, then right again to reach another bonfire. This is the one shown at the end of the abandoned swamp map. This fire will be guarded by several Shuju warriors, to whom parasites are attached. Destroy the parasites to be able to explore the area. Then find the path leading to the lighthouse. You'll meet another Shuju warrior down here, and before you enter the open area, you'll see an Umbral Flowerbed to the right. We recommend setting a checkpoint here using the seed as you are about to enter a new boss battle.

Boss Fight - The Silent Saint

The fight begins with the Silent Saint appearing on his horse and riding towards you. If you choose the right moment, you can block his attack and immediately knock him off his horse. If you dodge or miss an attack, he will move away and reappear. This time he will jump off his horse and his health bar will become visible and he will throw his weapon at you like a spear.

From this point on, you will be able to engage in combat or use ranged attacks. If you use melee combat, his attacks can be parried and blocked, allowing you to restore health and break his stance. If you use ranged attacks, he will most likely continue to throw his spear at you. Alternatively, he has a quick lunge attack, during which he will take a second to swing his spear back before lunging forward and covering a significant distance. The idea is to impale you with its weapon, which can kill you if you're too low on health.

If you use the Shadow Lamp, you will also notice vermin scattered around the battlefield. This can be used to summon spikes and knock down the Silent Saint, breaking his stance. If you do this multiple times, he will fall, allowing you to perform a Hard Kick. More and more of these parasites will spawn and spawn throughout the fight, so you don't have to worry about not having enough of them to carry you through the entire boss fight.

There are periods of time when you will be able to strike while he is recovering from attacks, but he will switch between melee and ranged attacks, as well as riding his horse. The most devastating attack he makes is when he rears his horse and it starts to glow blue/green. He will release a wave of spikes that covers a huge area of the arena. You can flip them over, jump over them, or just run away.

Second phase of the battle

When you reduce his health to half, he will also start calling his horse to attack. He will hit the shield and a horse will appear charging at you. He will continue to perform his attacks from the first phase of the fight, but will now also be able to throw out a wave of spikes without a horse.

After defeating the Saint, you will gain access to your first beacon and can clear it or leave it to burn. You will also receive 1 Remain Seed and 8 Shadow Purifiers. Enter the Umbral if you're not already there to hit the body and gain Shadow Cleanse and a flashback.

Once you have collected everything, head towards the fire-lit path and you will find the Remains of the Pale Butcher, where Teh-Ihir has now moved.

If you try to move forward, you will find a raised board that prevents you from moving. So, go left and smash the crates (you'll also see a body hanging above).

In this place you will find frog-like creatures that spew poison. There are quite a few of them, so expect them to attack you from all sides. Once you've cleared the area, knock the item off the hanging body to get a Panoptic Ring.

Turn left first and then look for a small gap on the left that will take you behind a rock. Here you can collect two items. Continue all the way to the left and break through the crates to collect 2 ammo bags and 2 mana stones. Follow the path until you reach the huts, go to the wooden path and go all the way to the left. Push the stairs down and take the item that is opposite - these are 3 poisonous salts.

Go straight to the slope and destroy the Shuja warrior. Continue up and watch out for Shuja to jump out at you from the right. Grab the 4 Deralium Fragments on the left and continue forward. Go down the stairs, then go left to knock down the plank and create a shortcut.

Stand in front of the board to find the path you'll need to follow to get to Fitzroy's Gulch. Continue through the cave until you reach a closed gate with a body next to it. Find the map of Fitzroy's Ravine, then use your Shadow Lamp to go through the gate. Descend between the mountains where you will meet hounds. To the right, one of them will burst through the forest and spit fire at you, so watch out for it.

Continue straight ahead and follow the Kalratha Trail to the right when you reach a fork. This will take you to the start of Fitzroy's Gorge as you reach the edge of the mountain.

Fitzroy Gorge

Fitzroy's Gorge is the seventh place you'll visit on your Mournstead journey. After finding the first of the beacons and clearing the swamp, the journey to Kalrath begins. In this section of our Lords of the Fallen walkthrough, we'll take you step-by-step through this new area and provide information on where to collect items, what enemies you'll encounter, and details on how to defeat the boss.

Start by walking down along the cliff. The first enemy you'll encounter is a sleeping dog, but you can catch it off guard with a heavy attack. As you pass the wooden barriers a little further ahead, you will encounter a dog walker who will try to catch you off guard.

You'll see a sleeping dog ahead, so you can use a heavy attack. Looking to the right, you can see a snake-like enemy with a crossbow on a raised platform, waiting for you.

When you start going down the slope, you will be attacked from afar. A hound will also run towards you. It's best to stand back and let the hound attack you to destroy it, then either use your own ranged attacks against the crossbow enemy or run past him. As you approach the ledge where the enemy with the crossbow is, you'll encounter another dog walker.

From here, go right and you will see another locked gate. Use your Shadow Lamp to go through here again and get to the other side. On the other side, a hound with a parasite is waiting for you. Use the Shadow Lamp to destroy the parasite and kill the dog.

Now go right and you will come to a room where three hounds will be sleeping. The dog walker will wander around, inspecting the area. If you are spotted, the hounds will wake up and attack, so approaching him unnoticed is a good attack option. Once you've cleared this area, go to the far right corner and pick up the Fitzroy Sword.

Here, switch to Umbral to go left and cross the bone bridge. Be careful, as creatures will fall on top of you and can throw you off the edge. Go left and use the Scarecrow to return to the Axiom. When you go down to the right of the Scarecrow, two dog walkers will be waiting for you (one roaming with a dog and the other on a wooden structure).

Head left from here to catch the snake-like ranged enemy trying to kill you when you first entered the cave, and another fire-breathing dog hiding behind some crates on the left. After defeating the snake-like enemy, take the item lying nearby. You can also go to Umbral here and hit the body on the opposite end of the cliff to create a shortcut, but it's best to stay in Axiom as you'll have a boss fight soon.

Go back the way you came, then go down the slope to the left. There will be a lot of hounds in this part of the cave that will eventually force you to come out. Once outside, continue down the slope to the left and when you try to cross the bridge, a battle with the Ruiner will begin.

Boss fight - Ruiner

The fight with Ruiner is quite difficult, since the action takes place on a bridge. This leaves you with little room to maneuver, locking you into a limited area with the boss. Going into this battle, you'll need to think about your ranged attacks and any items that will help you recover from fire damage or increase your resilience.

The Ruiner will start attacking you. If he hits any obstacle, he will be stopped, so try to keep the boxes that are initially on the bridge between you. This will give you the ability to attack using melee or ranged combat. Whatever you choose, he will start to push you towards the edge of the bridge, so you will have to dodge and start moving in the opposite direction to give yourself some space.

After dashing and jumping, he will set his weapon and shield on fire. This will allow him to leave trails of fire when using his weapon. You will then find that he will begin to perform various attack patterns in which he will emit waves of fire, or he will slam downwards and puddles of fire will begin to form around you, which will eventually explode. To top it off, he can also jump and lunge, creating a wide area of impact with his punches when landing.

Sometimes he throws a statue lit by fire next to him. Think of her as a parasite attached to the creatures in the game, and attack her whenever you can to deny the boss a boost.

His standard attacks can be parried and blocked, allowing you to regain health if you block and deal damage with Wither. Using Torment of Souls is also useful in this situation: it temporarily stops time so you can deal Drain damage to the Ruiner and remove its health once time speeds up again.

After winning, continue along Fitzroy's Gulch.

Walk to the end of the bridge, continuing through Fitzroy Gorge. Stop just after the arch and look up and to the right. Destroy the target here and it will allow you to go through the hole that is blocking the Umbral entity (on the left side if you look back the way you came).

Opposite the place where the Shadow Entity was blocking the doorway, a body will appear on another section of the bridge that needs to be acted upon. Do this to receive Nohut's Ritual Hammer. Now go to the Umbral doorway, jump down and go through it. Pull the platform and look up and to the right again. Destroy the body here to unblock the path before moving to the platform where the remains will appear.

Go up when you reach the end and go right first to lower the stairs. This will create a shortcut for you to climb up. Now go in the opposite direction to the building. Along the way you will encounter dog walkers, snake-like enemies and hounds.

Once you are in the building, go to the center and on the left you will find a bonfire, which is the Remains of Devoted Eliard. Continue to the center and look to the right. You will see a body in a chair, which is the Shrine of Adyr. You can use it for exchange. Interacting with him will give you a new gesture.

Go to the opening in the cave opposite the temple to collect the 3 Burnt Fingers from the body, then return to the bridge and cross it.

As you enter the new section of Fitzroy Gorge, you will see that the path goes down and to the right, but also up a bit. It will be blocked by wooden carts, but fight your way through them and go to the edge of the cliff to pick up the weighted bolts.

Now start going down the slope that will take you to the left. There is a body here where you can collect several items. At the bottom of the slope you will reach a fort, which is guarded by snake-like creatures, fire-breathing hounds and dog walkers. Kill them, then go to the tree on the far right and collect 2 Lesser Holy Salts, a Punishing Salt and a Bleeding Salt. Here you will also find a scarecrow that you can use if you are in Umbral.

Walk into the open courtyard and the Reaper of Light will appear.

Boss Fight - Reaper of Light

This fight can be quite challenging. If you fail to fight him here, you will die, respawn at the final bonfire, and be able to return to this area without him reappearing. So try, but don't be upset if you die.

Go to the place where the Reaper of Light appeared and go left. In the next area, you'll start to notice more enemies, ranging from enemies that can imbue their axes with fire attacks, to creatures that will throw firebombs at you.

Turn right and you will enter a graveyard where you will be attacked by many enemies using ranged fire. Follow the path through the left archway, then to the right, where a skeletal enemy with fire is patrolling. Enter the building on the left, go up the stairs, then go down. At the bottom of the stairs you will see a fire on the left and an item on the right. Pick up the Taxidermist's Hammer, then go left to the fire to begin the journey to Lower Kalrath.

Lower Kalrath

Lower Kalrath is the eighth area you'll come to on your journey through Mournstead. From the gorge you will go straight into the fire in Lower Kalrath.

When you first enter Lower Kalrath, you will see fire everywhere. The first place you will need to go is a path lined with flags where the fire is burning furiously. About halfway through you will see blue butterflies (if you are in Axiom) which indicate the presence of a stigma. Enter the Umbral and break through the stigma to see the memories play out and be rewarded with the Dark Crusader's Wooden Cross and 2x Umbral Purification.

Continue along the path and go around it to the right. Cross the bone bridge and go to the stairs in the burning building. Before going up the stairs, go to the right of them and grab the items. Climb the stairs and you will come to the next resting place - Sebastian's Remains.

From here, go left and left again to the flag. There is a ledge here that you can jump onto, which has a Sky Vial on it that you can pick up. Go back and continue left. You will see a broken wooden platform with an item on the other side. Run across it and jump to pick up the map of Lower Kalrath.

Walk along the wooden path and go down the stairs. Go forward and take 3 salts from the corner. Then go right along the path to the broken bridge, where you will enter an area surrounded by fire and fight the boss - the Infernal Enchantress.

Boss Fight - Infernal Sorceress

When the fight begins, a red protective bubble will immediately appear around the Enchantress. Additionally, there will be a blue orb on the panel, indicating that it is protected by parasites.

Some of your ranged attacks will be able to penetrate this red protective barrier, but you need to break it quickly in order for your attacks to be more effective. To do this you need to find four parasites. While you're determining where they are, focus on ranged attacks to make the most of your time.

If you go to the beginning of the arena, you will find a parasite hanging over the wooden walkway. You can find the second one nearby, near the wall. The third parasite can be found on the left near the broken bridge. The last one is right next to him, near the tree.

Once the barrier is destroyed, you will be able to choose between melee and ranged attacks. If you stick to ranged combat, you'll see her throwing fireballs at you. When she gets ready to throw a fireball, she will reach back and it will hold for a moment before launching the projectile at you.

In addition, she performs attacks in which red lines appear and fireballs rise along them from the ground. You need to dodge them to avoid taking damage. Sometimes when they explode, the Enchantress will immediately throw a fireball at you, which is quite difficult to see, so it's best to always assume that she will continue this attack and roll to the side.

If you prefer melee combat and are close to the Enchantress, be prepared for her moveset to change quickly. She will envelop herself in a whirlpool of fire, which will gradually increase and eventually explode. This can take a lot of your health, so run when this happens. At the end of the explosion, she will disappear and reappear somewhere else in the arena. Apart from this, she will also use her arm as a flamethrower, chasing you wherever you go.

When the fight is over, you will receive the Seed, Infernal Sorceress Flesh, Infernal Sorceress Flail, and Infernal Sorceress Helm.

After killing the Infernal Enchantress, go behind the tree and look to the right. Behind the flames there is an alley hidden from prying eyes. Follow it to the end, turning left to pick up the Magma Ring.

Return to the tree and go to the opposite side of this alley to find a ladder that will lead you up. As you go upstairs, you will see enemies passing by. First, go left and look behind the wooden barricade to the left of the door. Here you can take the cultist's pyric flail from the body.

Now go up the path and you will come to a small wooden staircase on the right. This will lead you to the scarecrow. Continue along the path and look for wooden barrels and crates on the right as the path begins to climb to the left. Break through them and go behind the building along the slope on the right. Below, if you look to the other side of the yard, you will see a dog walker on the balcony of another building. If you're in Axiom, this will seem like a dead end since the bridge is broken, but head into Umbral and across the bone bridge to reach the dog walker. Go right and follow the path to an opening in the building that will lead you to a ladder that is right next to Sabastian's Remains, so lower it to reveal a shortcut.

Drop down and go up the stairs again, this time going up the slope to the left. As you go up, you will see a snake-like enemy with a crossbow. But beware of the dog hiding behind the wooden beams on the right when you reach the first building.

Continue up the slope to the left and you'll pass a scarecrow. Then go right and through the barricades. Further along the path, another skeleton knight will appear, wielding fire. Once in the next section, go down the steps and look to the left to see moths floating in the gap between two buildings. Enter Umbral, then pull up the platform. Cross to the other side and look up to see a creature ready to pounce on you. Jump down to the left, then go up the stairs and use the scarecrow to return to the Axiom.

Go to the right of the scarecrow and go up the stairs, where you will meet another Infernal Enchantress. Turn right again and look down at the dog walker sitting on the roof. Enter the Umbral, then look to the left and use your abilities on the body to extend the bridge. He won't stay put, so you'll need to quickly get back to him and hit the body on the other side to cross the gap.

On the other side, use the scarecrow to return to the Axiom. Start walking towards the bridge to the left of the scarecrow, then watch out for the fiery enemies that will quickly attack you from the right. In addition, you will also have to deal with a dog walker with a firearm sitting on the other side of the bridge. Go to the left of it and then turn right to be in the next section. At the top of the stairs is the next bonfire you can activate - the Remains of Lydia, the Numb Witch, and right in front of them there is an item to collect - the Kalrath Slums Map.

Slums of Kalrath

The Kalrath Slums are the eighth area you'll come to on your journey through Mournstead.

From the Remains of Lydia, the Numb Witch, go right. Jump to the ledge below and go down the stairs to the next section.

Look to the right of the stairs and pick up the items, which will give you a Prol's Hat, a Prol's Clothes, a Prol's Wrap, and a Prol's Pants.

Now head down where you will come to a room where an enemy will appear and an open gate leading outside. When you start walking here, look down and you will see some bombs lying on the ground. You'll need to avoid them as you fall down, and be prepared to quickly roll out of the way to avoid being hit by their explosions. The easiest way to do this is to get down as close to the ledge you're on as possible. You should be able to completely avoid the first bomb and then slowly move forward.

Follow the path and find the first plank on the left, where a snake-like enemy is waiting to pounce on you with his crossbow. Continue along this path, breaking the wooden carts to get through. At the end you will see an arch that is not completely filled with bricks. Before you reach it, check the left side: a hound will jump at you. There is also a staircase that will take you to the left, but go through the archway first.

Use your Shadow Lamp here to go through it and up the stairs. In this room you will find a chest containing several items: a Leather and Tooth Sword, 2 Fire Salts, 2 Holy Salts and 2 Withering Salts.

Leave this area and go up the stairs to the right (which were on the left when you entered here). Climb up and walk until you reach a hole in the building. Break the boxes and jump down. In this area, you need to get to the bottom as quickly as possible, since all the enemies here are protected by parasites.

There is one large pest down there, so jump down there and destroy it to make all the enemies vulnerable to your attacks. Take the time to clear them out, then pick up your Shadow Lamp and head to the hole in the wall at the bottom of the stairs. Go through to collect the items from the dog walker's body.

Go back up the stairs and you will see a broken board in the hole in the wall. You will be able to run and jump to get to the other side. From the board you're currently on you'll see that it's connected to other buildings burning around, but if you continue down this path you'll miss important parts of this area with good loot, so jump down onto the beam and destroy the snake-like creature , going straight through the archway to prevent it from hitting you as you continue to explore the area.

Go back to where the bombs were when you first fell into this area and go up the left side (right if you're facing away from the gate where you fell towards the bombs). Here you will see a dog walker. Go up the small ladder, then go left to smash the crates as shown in the picture above. Go to the end of the alley and take 2 ammo bags and 2 small manastone clusters from the body.

From here, go left and break through the pot to reach a dead end. There will be a body with a Guardian amulet here that you can pick up.

Return to the entrance and then go through the next arch where the snake-like creature was. Smash the wooden carts that are blocking your progress here and go down the stairs. You will come to a large bonfire where the Destroyer is located. There are several key items here, including the Antediluvian Chisel, so it's worth taking the time to clear out all the enemies here.

When you first enter this area, run to the right and grab the items. To obtain the Antediluvian Chisel, you need to enter the Umbral. This will also cause a Lying Face to spawn, so it's best to clear out as much of the area as possible before entering the Umbral. You then need to look for a body on the bonfire that you can interact with to get the chisel.

Go up the stairs, break the crates on the left and be prepared for the hound that will run at you. At the other end of the bridge, use the scarecrow to get back, then climb up to the roof using the slope to the left. Head to the board directly opposite the small roof to knock it down and explore the burning buildings. It will connect with the previous ones, so you won't miss anything.

Cross the board and turn right first. Here you will encounter fire dogs and their remains roaming around, so be careful while exploring. Look to the right to see some boxes on the balcony. Break these boxes to obtain Adyr's Mark Ring. Now go to the opposite side, where the fire is raging. Open the door on the right and enter Umbral.

Cleanse the soul on the stigma to get 2 Shadow Cleanses here, then go right and collect the Slag Bolts. Go back to where you originally came from on the rooftops, then go up to the next rooftop on the left. Go right and up to find a room containing 2 common Deralium Nuggets, then go back and turn right.

You'll see slanted roofs on the right and a bridge on the left. You can either jump down or cross to the other side and go down the stairs. As you move into the next section, you will see another bonfire in the distance, guarded by the Enchantress. There will be a wooden structure on the right.

As soon as you enter this area, a dog walker will run towards you from this wooden structure. Kill him and go upstairs to face another enemy. After defeating him too, enter the Umbral to go up the stairs.

Walk to the end, then turn right and enter the building. On the left, as soon as you enter, you can pick up 2 regular Deralium Nuggets. Get to the end and follow the path to the next building. Head back and use the Scarecrow to leave Umbral, then go down the stairs on the left. This will allow you to get past the Enchantress at the campfire.

Once off the ledge, look to the right and find another wall that you can pass through using the Shadow Lamp. Enter here and pick up the Jagged Staff. Once back outside, go up the slope to the right and ignore the wall of fire to the left. Instead, go straight up to fight a skeleton knight.

Enter the room behind it and go up the stairs to reach the top. Enter the Umbral to see an invisible wall on the right. Go through it to find a chest containing the Lava Burst spell. Now go left from the stairs and you will see a dog walker sitting on the edge. Just before you reach him, grab the 2 Weak Energy Skulls from the body on the right.

Head towards the dog walker and throw him off to easily deal with him. The path you need to take goes to the right, but look left first to see planks that can be broken. Follow there and around the corner you will meet an enemy. Once the enemies are dead, go across the bridge to get to the other side. Be prepared to destroy the Maw of Despair guarding the body you can interact with. By doing this, you will receive Holy Quintessence.

Go down the stairs and look to the right to see a bell. Behind the bell, in the corner, wooden beams are burning. Approach them and take the Sword of the Fallen Lord. Take the stairs all the way down to the bottom and you will see that they lead to the stairs you climbed and passed by the skeleton knight. This is a room covered in a wall of flames, so go through the door opposite the one that will lead you back up the stairs. Go all the way to the dead end to collect things from the bodies.

Now, instead of going up the stairs again, go up, cross the bridge and climb to the top of the structure. There are enemies waiting for you in the first room, so take them out and then go up the stairs to the next section.

Here you will meet two dogs. Once you've dealt with them, look behind the breakable barrels in the corner to find the Blackfeather Ranger's Axe. To continue, you need to re-enter the Umbral, go up the stairs and get to the stairs that will take you out of this section. When you come out of the stairs you need to move straight forward, but there are some items you need to collect in this area first.

Turn around and look at the opposite end of the stairs to use the Scarecrow to exit the Umbral and return to the Axiom. Then go right and break the crates to reach the passage on the other side of the buildings and take the Ring of Power from the body.

Now continue along the path, killing the Enchantress, and go down the stairs. When you do this, you will see a giant and an arena that will show you what you will have to face in your next boss fight.

Boss Fight - Rejected Offspring

In this fight, avoid locking onto the target. Since you can capture several areas, from his arms to his legs and head. Due to the size of the boss, locking can affect the camera angle and mean you'll miss important cues about when his attack will begin.

You'll have to dodge a lot of attacks in the first phase, but no matter what he does, you need to spend this part of the fight attacking his legs. Here are the attacks that can await you:

- He will bring his arms down, scratching the arena and leaving lava claw marks. You'll need to avoid these areas while trying to attack his legs, but luckily this attack is easy to dodge.

- He will try to hit you, usually by swiping his finger. His arms are long, so his strikes cover a large area of the arena, but you can dodge this strike. Sometimes these blows are followed by the boss slamming both hands onto the ground in front of him, exposing his back and leaving his legs vulnerable. It will take him a while to come to his senses, so hit his legs as many times as you can during these moments.

- He will raise his head to the sky and a hand will appear, releasing fireballs. This attack also has a variation where he will perform attacks similar to Infernal Enchantress's and lines will appear from the ground causing explosions. They will follow you wherever you are, so just roll away from them when they appear.

45

- From time to time he lifts one leg up, which indicates that he is about to fall to the ground while trying to mount you. This can happen quite quickly, so you need to dodge as soon as you see him lift his leg. He gets up pretty quickly too, so there's no point in trying to attack his legs when that happens.
- Finally, he will try to punch the ground where you are. This is usually one punch with each hand and then a move where he slams both fists into the ground.

The goal of this phase of the fight is to reduce his health until he stops, leans forward, and starts spewing lava. It will cover the entire floor, making the lower part of the arena impossible to use. Instead, you will need to climb up any stairs and take a position on one of the shafts above to begin the second stage of the fight.

Second phase of the battle

This phase requires patience as you will have to do a lot of dodging and only certain boss attacks will give you the opportunity to land multiple hits. However, the attacks he uses in this battle are repetitive, so it's all about identifying which attacks are about to happen in order to prepare to respond.

The first attack you'll see is him slamming each hand. When this happens, you need to roll as he starts to lower his hand and try to get close to it so that you can hit his hand at least once. This is usually followed by a swipe attack that you need to roll to dodge.

Things get a little more complicated when he starts repeating the fire attack, slamming his fist and releasing a wave of fire. Just like in the first phase, roll towards him. This is actually the move where you'll be able to land the most hits, as it will take him a while to raise his arm again. You should have 4 to 5 hits, especially if you happen to be nearby at that moment.

In addition to these attacks, he will also squat so that his face is parallel to the shaft you are standing on. When he does this, he is going to shoot his fist out of his mouth and try to catch you. He'll do this three times, so just roll away from those attacks. You'll know when the hand is about to come out as there is a faint roar before each attack.

You then have two attack options where he raises his head and his hand comes out of his mouth. The first attack you can see is spitting fireballs. This means running away as he is going to cover the shaft you are on with lava, meaning it will be temporarily unusable. All you need to do to do this is move to another shaft.

Another attack that starts the same way is a huge fireball attack. It will begin to lean back, while the ball will burn brightly, and the area around you will turn red. You'll start taking fire damage if you stay near him for too long, so run to both sides of the rampart and hide behind the wall. Eventually, the ball will end with a huge explosion.

At this point, once you deal enough damage, he will grab his throat and lean back. It will temporarily remain in place, and the lava will disappear from the lower level. Once this happens, run down and land the final blows needed to finish the fight.

Once the boss falls, you will receive a Seed, 8 Dark Purification, Forsaken Offspring Flesh, and a Giant Eyeball.

If you're not already in Umbral, you should use the altar-facing stigma here if possible. This will give you 2x Dark Cleanse and Boss Flashback.

After the fight, if you encounter Stigma and the statue, go right and look for two statues on the pillars. Behind the right you can find 3 salts. Now go left from the stigma and the statue. Climb the stairs and you will reach the next bonfire - Doln's Remains.

Upper Kalrath Mining District

The Upper Kalrath Mining District is the tenth district you'll come to on your journey through Mournstead. While the rest of Kalrath is in flames, the mining district of Upper Kalrath is covered in ash.

From Doln's Remains, go right and through the open gate. Before you go to the other side, take out the Shadow Lamp and use it to go through the grate on the left.

Go to the end and take the Upper Kalrath Mining District Map from the body. Exit the grate using the Shadow Lamp, then go left.

Follow the path, destroying fiery remains along the way. Pick up the Justicar's Tincture, which you will see on the body on the left when you first enter this area. When you reach the gate with two figures in front of it, go left. More fiery remnants will appear and you need to start making your way to the right.

Don't go all the way to the right, instead look for a blocked staircase on the right with two more ash figures next to it. Use the Shadow Lamp to go through the gate, then look down to the right to see where you need to go. Before you jump down, be aware that behind the boarded up hole in the wall is a dog walker protected by a parasite, so pick up your Shadow Lamp and destroy him before the enemy jumps out. Jump and attack the dog walker, then pick up the object from the body - a contemptuous scarecrow. Go left and climb up the cart, then use your Shadow Lamp again to get back up.

Go left to the boxes. Again, there will be a dog walker here with a vermin ready to pounce on you. So deal with him before collecting the 3 Lesser Holy Salts. Then go right, take out the enemy with ranged attacks in the doorway and pick up the Old Mornstead Greatsword.

Go left again and a mage protected by a parasite awaits you at the end of the balcony. Go through the first archway on the left to enter an alcove and grab some supplies.

As soon as you approach the mage, a skeleton knight wielding fire will appear on the left side and will try to knock you down. There will also be other enemies here that will attack you. When you manage to clear this area, you should move to Umbral. Look at the place where the magician stood so that you can run up and jump over the broken bridge that appears and search the hanging body. This will give you the Parting Pendant.

Now jump down and go right. You can exit Umbral here through the scarecrow under the broken bridge. You will find two more magicians and a dog walker who is protected by a parasite. Destroy the parasites and then clear the area. Look for the stairs leading to the courtyard, but be sure to climb them.

When you head into the courtyard with the tree in the middle, be aware that there is an Infernal Sorceress leading a group of enemies. You need to carefully kill them so that you can explore the area. Start in a tree where you can knock down a body and pick up an item. Then look at the boxes in the corner by the tree and break them.

Now enter the Umbral to be able to hit the body on the side of the building and receive the Holy Quintessence. Climb the next set of stairs and find a dead end on the right, where at the end lies the body of a dog walker that you can search. Now follow the path to the left and at the top it will be a dead end. Drop down the hole on the right which will lead you into the building and open the door to continue.

Grab the item on the bookshelf straight ahead, then go left. You'll go down the stairs to a room with a fireplace, a mage, and a skeleton knight. Kill them, then enter the Umbral to interact with Stigma, which will give you consumables.

Grab the Shattered Runic Tablet from the fireplace, then ignore the path going left. Instead, go back to the stairs and go through this door (it connects to the path that the door to the left of the fireplace will take you to).

You will enter a room where a spiral slope goes up and down. First go upstairs and there you will find a chest with Warden Pants, Warden Clothes, Warden Mask and Warden Gloves inside.

Now go to the end and enter the room. Walk to the edge of the platform on the left and break the boxes to collect 4 small deralium fragments. Look down and kill the mage, then start going up the stairs on the right. Hit the body hanging from the beam where the magician is, and the object will fall to the very bottom of the room. Go down there to collect it and get the Warden's Halberd.

Kill the two cross enemies here, then pull the lever to open the gate. Grab the Dark Skane Map from the body near the book on the right, then follow the tracks. When the road splits, you will see a door on the left. It can't be opened unless you have the key, so go right and activate the Hooded Remains of Antuli before you start exploring Dark Skein.

Dark Skane

This is the eleventh location you will come to on your journey through Mournstead.

From the Remains of the Hooded Antuli, go right. Enter the room and take out the enemies with crosses, then look at the ledge on the left and you will see a mage protected by a parasite. Use your Shadow Lamp to destroy the parasite, then continue on.

You will come to a closed gate, but first look to the right to collect 4 small deralium fragments. Then start moving left from the closed gate. Go up the stairs and turn right to go further into the mines.

As you walk down this hallway, you'll see an enemy wandering up and down, but watch out for one who surprises you by jumping over the breakable crates to the left. Inside this niche you can collect 4 small fragments of deralium.

Continue towards the magician and turn right. You will see another closed gate and moths in front of you. Before going through the gate, use the Shadow Lamp to grab the 4 small Deralium Fragments from the body to the right of the gate.

At the end of the corridor you need to turn right, but first break the boxes in front of you to collect 2 poison cures. Now go right and be ready to rush back when the enemy rolls a barrel on you. Head towards the mage and just before you reach him the floor will give way and you will fall to the bottom of the shaft.

Beware of headless creatures that can poison you with their attacks, and once the area is clear, pick up the Ancient Amulet from the body. Continue through this flooded corridor until you reach the end of the ledge. Attack the mage on the other side, then enter the Umbral to reach the other side and turn right.

Destroy the stigma in the upper left to obtain consumables as you enter the next room, then use the scarecrow to exit the Umbral. Now go up the stairs on the right and use the beam to keep going up until you reach the broken section.

At the top, destroy the magician and the enemy with the cross, then continue on your way. Break through the wooden beams. Pick up the Ring of the First of the Beasts from the body, then go left along the paths. At the end of this platform, two enemies will break through the wooden planks ahead and try to surprise you. Once you defeat them, go right, go down the stairs and pull the lever.

Don't go down the stairs, but go to the end of the ledge where the two enemies were hiding. Look down and to the right, then jump down. Pick up the upgraded fire grenade and drop down again. You will be returned to the beginning of the level, but now the gate that was initially closed will be raised.

Go through the open gate and you will see new enemies with pickaxes, as well as a mage. Collect the 2 common Deralium Nuggets on the right as soon as you enter this section. Look to the left to see a ladder and go up there.

Defeat the enemies in the first room you come to and go straight from the door to collect 1 Ammo Bag and 2 Manastone Chunks. From the scarecrow, you can go left and straight to find a mage and another enemy, or go up the stairs opposite him. If you go up the stairs, it will lead you to the place where you fell and where the magician used to be. Now you will be able to get the bolts he has.

Go back down and go left from the scarecrow to the mage, then grab the item from the crates next to the mage. Leave this area, return to the stairs, but before going down them, look for a hanging broken platform.

Jump over here, follow the path to the end and take the Fulvirano Shield from the body. Now go down the stairs and head towards the closed gate. You won't be able to open them from this side, so follow the corridor to the right and go all the way until you reach the next closed gate. Use the Shadow Lamp to get through them.

There are two paths in the next room, but the easiest is ahead, behind the barrels that you can crash through (they'll both merge later anyway). Enter Umbral, then drop down to the ledge below. Destroy the body in the blocked doorway to reveal a stigma. Interact with her, then collect 2 regular Deralium nuggets.

Now go in the opposite direction and turn right when you get to the end (going left will take you back to where you just were). Continue forward, then when you enter the section with the green mist, look to the right and pick up the Whisper Shield. Continue and you'll come to a room guarded by the Womb of Despair. There are two items to collect in this room: on the right you can get a Rot and on the left you can get an Energy Skull.

Go up the stairs in the next room and pick up the Animated Energy Skull opposite the scarecrow, then use it to exit the Umbral. Continue up the stairs, get rid of the enemies with crosses at the top and follow the mine corridor. When you exit, look for a parasite-protected enemy with a cross. Go right, run up to this platform and take them out so they don't attack you while exploring.

This time, go back down and to the left, where you will be on the other side of the door that you were unable to open earlier. Take out the two enemies with pickaxes, then grab 4 small Deralium fragments on the left, and then on the right, just before the door, another 4 small Deralium fragments. Open the door to create a shortcut for yourself.

Now you need to enter the Umbral and go to the broken edge to the right of the door you opened. Look towards the center of the room and use your abilities to move the platform. This will allow you to use the stairs in the center of the room to reach the next bonfire. Climb the stairs and head back to the bonfire that will be visible when you reach the top.

Just before this, you will also be able to use the effigy to leave Umbral, but you can use Katrina's Remains and rest instead. You will meet Byron again, who will give you a mourning gesture as soon as you talk to him. You'll need to use the remains to rest and level up before doing anything else in the main room. The door behind Byron is locked, so you still have to return to it.

Leave the fire and follow the path on the left. Now that you are in the Axiom, you will be able to see a mechanism located next to the stairs you climbed. Use it to drain the water below. Go down and run around to collect all the Energy Skulls from the bodies on the floor.

Return to the beginning of the location and go under the platform with the magician and the enemy with the cross. You can now cross the gate and get to the other side of this area. Go through them, then turn left to knock down the plank and build a bridge that will take you back to the bonfire.

Now go in the direction opposite the bridge and be prepared for the barrels to roll down and possibly hit you. A little higher up there is a skeleton knight. Once you reach the end of this shaft, you will enter a room with a snake-like enemy using a crossbow.

When you enter this room, there will also be hounds ready to jump on you. Look to the left, by the closed gate, to find a chest containing Sovereign Defender Gauntlets, Sovereign Defender Leggings, Sovereign Defender Armor, and Sovereign Defender Helm.

Now go up the stairs to the right and follow the path until you reach a dead end. Use your Shadow Lamp to get through this gate too. Once you reach the top, find the mage on the opposite side and destroy the parasite so you can attack him. A skeleton knight is waiting for you below, but try to jump and attack him to deprive him of half his health with one blow.

Go down the stairs and you'll see a path going to the left and a ladder straight ahead. Go straight ahead to lower the ladder first, then take the path leading left. Go up the stairs and you'll end up where the mage was just before, go to the end of this path and pick up the Cursed Effigy from the body, then jump down.

Go straight first, then defeat the dog walker and take the Ring of Berinon from the body on the right. Turn to face the other way and go to the magician near the lever. First, look to the left and pick up the Shadow Lamp to reveal a parasite that you will need to destroy to make enemies in the area vulnerable. You will meet several dog walkers, hounds and magicians.

Pull the lever, then jump down or use the ladder to reach the bottom of the room. The gate that was previously closed near the chest will now be open. Look at the tracks to find the book and pick up the map of the Kalrath Cisterns from it.

Go back up the stairs and use the Shadow Lamp to approach the body on the metal boxes (to the left as you go up the stairs) and take the key. Then go down and go through the archway to enter the Kalrath Cistern.

Kalrath tank

Kalrath Cistern is the twelfth location you will come to on your journey through Mournstead.

You will be taken to the Kalrath Cistern. If you followed our walkthrough, you will pick up the map to this location in the last room, and also pick up the key from the body on the cells. The entrance to the Kalrath Cistern is directly through the door next to the body.

Follow the corridor to the left, where you will encounter a dog and a snake-like enemy with a crossbow. At the end of this corridor you will need to go right and go up the stairs. This will lead you to some steps blocked at the top and a small area to the left. Here you will fight your next boss, the Skin Snatcher.

Boss Fight – Skin Snatcher

The boss fight takes place in such a confined space that you have virtually no chance of moving. Luckily, this is a fairly easy fight. The boss has four arms, each with an attack blade. However, he will often attack only one of them or perform a combination of two attacks and stop for a moment to pause before starting to attack again.

His typical attack is just one simple punch that you can dodge, parry, or block. When this happens, you can only land 1 to 2 hits as he will skid, stop and take time to recover. Such a blow will also break his stance and give you the opportunity to interrupt him. Just try not to get too greedy with your attacks, as he may immediately start attacking you again.

The worst attack the boss does is the one where he charges up his blades and quickly sets them on fire. There isn't much time between the start of the attack and the time he lunges forward to cut you. As soon as he raises his hands and a glow appears, get ready to dodge as he will quickly rush at you.

As he lunges forward and sticks out the blade, it will be followed by another quick strike. If you stay close to the boss and roll when he attacks, you will be able to stay close to him and hit him immediately. Whenever combos occur, he will perform a maximum of two hits, so be prepared to dodge and roll away from each one. Even if you reduce his health below half, his attack pattern will remain the same.

For defeating the Skin Snatcher you will receive a seed, a Drainage Control Room Key, a Skin Snatcher Armor and a Skin Snatcher Cleaver.

When the fight is over, open the door behind and pull the lever on the right. This will activate the elevator, which will take you to Upper Kalrath. First of all, go to Umbral and look for the body behind on the left. Pick up an item.

Go to Upper Kalrath or go to Depths of Revelation.

Here you can skip the entire area and take the elevator to Upper Kalrath. However, if you continue exploring the Kalrath Cistern and descend into the Depths of Revelation, there will be plenty of loot and a few additional bosses waiting for you. For the purposes of this walkthrough, we will be exploring the Depths of Revelation.

Go down the stairs back to the previous location. Don't turn around to where the snake-like enemy and the dog are, but continue down towards the dog walker. Destroy the parasite that protects it, and then clear the platform. Look to the right of the stairs to see a series of platforms that exist in Umbral.

Jump onto the first and second, then run and jump over the next three. You'll see a reaper-like enemy below, but you won't be able to attack him from here. This is actually an optional boss fight, so if you're going to continue, you might want to see how to deal with it.

Additional boss fight - Bringer of Calm, Bringer of Nothingness and Bringer of Silence

The first figure you'll see on the platforms above is the Bringer of Tranquility. From this platform, perform a jump and an attack move. This will effectively reduce his health to half before the fight even begins. As you explore Umbral up to this point, you will see that these enemies become more and more common, so you should already be familiar with their attack types. Fortunately, these attack patterns remain the same in combat.

Be prepared for a second enemy, the Bringer of Nothingness, to appear as soon as you remove half of the Bringer of Tranquility's health. If you use beeps, you will begin to hear a hum-like noise. You'll have a brief moment where you can continue to target the Bringer of Tranquility before a second Bringer will jump up from the ground and try to stab you with both blades.

It's a good idea to try to continue focusing your attacks on the Bringer of Tranquility and simply dodge the second enemy's attacks. If you can, try to position them as close together as possible so that you can hit them both at the same time. When you are almost done with the Bringer of Calm, a third enemy will appear - the Bringer of Silence. This is why you need to finish off the Tranquility Bringer first so you can only deal with two enemies at a time rather than all three.

The most dangerous attack to watch out for is when they disappear onto a platform and you'll see a black, smokey path from where they move underground. Pay close attention to this and the screaming sound that plays just before they pounce on you.

In addition, they usually jump back and then spin and attack. If you're dealing with all these attacks, they'll usually follow each other, meaning you'll have to block or dodge three attacks in a row - another reason why it's easier to fight two enemies. If you dodge and roll out of the way, the target lock can sometimes take you right off the edge of that platform. And since you're in Umbral, that means you'll die outright.

Gradually kill the bosses, focusing your attacks on one of them.

When the battle is over, you will receive the Left Sword of the Bringer of Tranquility, a Hood, a Seed of Remains, and 5 Shadow Purification.

Now you will need to hit the body opposite this platform to create a bridge. Cross over and smash the body in the wall to get Marco's Axe, then go left to the end of the stairs. This appears to be a dead end, but look down and jump to the platform below to enter the pipes.

This area goes in many different directions so it can be confusing, but we recommend you approach it as follows. Clean the first area of any remaining eggs. Go to the end of this hallway, where you'll see a door on the right, a section straight ahead, and a hallway going off to the left with lots of holes.

Go left first, but ignore the first hole on the left. Instead, go all the way. Clear out the enemies here, grab the 2 Poison Medicines from the grate on the right, and interact with the body to get a Nohuta Effigy. Leave this area, now go to the door that was originally on your right (now opposite you). Walk to the edge of the platform and jump down, then turn right.

You'll see that this path also ends, but go straight first and ignore the tunnel on the left for now. Climb the stairs and be prepared to meet a dog walker at the top who will throw a barrel at you when you reach the top. Collect 3 Flammable Salts from the body of the butcher you pass, then continue into the next room. First, go to the alcove on the right, but be prepared for another dog walker to jump out at you. Kill him, then look to the right to grab an ammo bag and 2 mana stones, and then to the left to open the door - this will take you back to Kalrath Depths, where you first entered the Kalrath Cistern.

Return to the previous room and go down the stairs to the Scarecrow. Return to the Axiom, then go to the grate where the skeleton is to collect the Unblinking Root. Turn around and push the ladder down, then go down it.

You'll be back where you first entered this section, in the room that was first on the left. Now follow the path that is directly in front of you when you get off the stairs. Beware of the archer here, who will move quickly and frequently while invisible. You can spot him by the bright green lights that appear, which will always show you where he is. It can be hit even when invisible, so just watch out for the green light.

Get to the end of this hallway, then go up the next set of stairs, which is on the right. Look ahead and you will see a locked door with a lever behind it. Here you will use the key to the drainage control room obtained from the Skin Thief, but first you need to deal with the hidden dangers that await you on the right side of this room.

If you look to the right, you will see a broken wall. Behind there is a skeleton protected by a parasite, and shortly before that, behind the wooden barrels, a dog is waiting for you. Kill the dog first and pick up your Shadow Lamp to destroy the parasite before the skeleton even appears. Kill enemies to reveal a secret room.

Follow the path into the room and to the altar, but beware of another dog walker that will jump out of you. When it is safe to do so, go to the Umbral, if you are not already in it, interact with the stigma and you will receive two Shadow Cleanses. Then take the saw from the altar.

Now open the door with the Drainage Control Room Key and take the Sky Vial on the right. Then pull the lever to drain the water. Go down the stairs to where the archer was and go left. Go through the door and jump off the ledge again. This time, instead of going straight, turn left into the tunnel. Take 2 salts and go to the end of the tunnel. Now that the water has been drained, bodies, cells and objects that were previously hidden will now be at the bottom.

Jump off from here, go along the cells and take the first item from the raft - 3 ordinary deralium nuggets. Then continue following the cage to the body in front of the pipe. Grab 3 ammo bags and 2 large manastone clusters and if you continue down this pipe you will reach the Depths of Revelation.